Working Papers
for use with
Financial Accounting
A Business Perspective

Seventh Edition

Roger H. Hermanson
Georgia State University

James Don Edwards
University of Georgia

**Irwin
McGraw-Hill**

Boston   Burr Ridge, IL   Dubuque, IA   Madison, WI   New York   San Francisco   St. Louis
Bangkok   Bogotá   Caracas   Lisbon   London   Madrid
Mexico City   Milan   New Delhi   Seoul   Singapore   Sydney   Taipei   Toronto

Irwin/McGraw-Hill

A Division of The McGraw-Hill Companies

Working Papers for use with
FINANCIAL ACCOUNTING: A BUSINESS PERSPECTIVE

1 2 3 4 5 6 7 8 9 0 BBC/BBC 9 0 9 8 7

ISBN 0-07-289141-6

http://www.mhhe.com

Exercise 1-1

1. _____ 2. _____ 3. _____ 4. _____ 5. _____ 6. _____

Exercise 1-2

a. _____

b. _____

Exercise 1-3

a. _____

b. _____

Exercise 1-4

_____

_____

_____

Exercise 1-5

a. _____

b. _____

c. _____

d. _____

e. _____

f. _____

Exercise 1-6

BRADLEY COMPANY
Summary of Transactions
Month of July 1999

Trans-action	Explanation	Assets				=	Liabilities		+	Stockholders' Equity	
		Cash	Accounts Receivable	Trucks	Office Equipment =		Accounts Payable	Notes Payable +		Capital Stock	Retained Earnings
a.											
b.											
c.											
d.											
e.											
f.											
g.											
h.											
i.											

Exercise 1-7

a. _____

b. _____

c. _____

d. _____

e. _____

Exercise 1-8

a. _____
b. _____
c. _____
d. _____
e. _____
f. _____

Exercise 1-9

_____
_____
_____

Exercise 1-10

CINCK COMPANY
Income Statement
For the Month Ended July 31,1999

Exercise 1-11

BRINDLE COMPANY
Statement of Retained Earnings
For the Month Ended August 31,1999

SPEEDY PRINTER REPAIR, INC
Balance Sheet
December 31,1999

Assets										Liabilities and Stockholders' Equity																			

Exercise 1-13

Problem 1-1

PRESTON AUTO PAINT COMPANY
Summary of Transactions
Month of September 1999

Date	Explanation	Assets			Liabilities	Stockholders' Equity	
		Cash	Accounts Receivable	Equipment	Accounts Payable	Capital Stock	Retained Earnings

Chapter 1

Problem 1-1A

LAKEWOOD PERSONAL FINANCE COMPANY
Summary of Transactions
Month of May 1999

Date	Explanation	Assets			=	Liabilities	+	Stockholders' Equity	
		Cash	Accounts Receivable	Equipment		Notes Payable		Capital Stock	Retained Earnings

Problem 1-2 or 1-2A

a.

Summary of Transactions
Month of _____ 1999

Date	Explanation	Assets			Liabilities	Stockholders' Equity	
		Cash	Accounts Receivable		Payable	Capital Stock	Retained Earnings

_____

Balance Sheet

_____ 30, 1999

Assets

Liabilities and Stockholders' Equity

Name _____

_____

_____

Income Statement

For the _____ Ended June 30, 1999

Problem 1-3A

b.   **MOONLIGHT DRIVE-IN THEATER**

Statement of Retained Earnings

For the Month Ended June 30, 1999

MOONLIGHT DRIVE-IN THEATER

Balance Sheet

June 30, 1999

Assets

Liabilities and Stockholders' Equity

d.

Business Decision Case 1-1   Name _____

_____

_____
_____
_____
_____
_____
_____
_____
_____
_____
_____
_____
_____
_____
_____
_____
_____
_____
_____
_____
_____
_____
_____
_____
_____
_____
_____
_____
_____
_____
_____
_____
_____
_____
_____
_____

Annual Report Analysis 1-2

_____
_____
_____
_____
_____
_____
_____
_____
_____
_____

Annual Report Analysis 1-3

Name_____

_____
_____
_____
_____
_____
_____
_____
_____
_____
_____
_____
_____
_____
_____
_____
_____
_____
_____
_____
_____
_____
_____

Ethics Case–Writing Experience 1-4

_____
_____
_____
_____
_____
_____
_____
_____
_____
_____
_____
_____
_____
_____
_____
_____
_____
_____
_____
_____
_____
_____
_____

Name _____

Exercise 2-6

a. _____
b. _____
c. _____
d. _____
e. _____
f. _____
g. _____
h. _____
i. _____
j. _____

Exercise 2-7

TUXEDOS, INC.

Trial Balance

December 31, 1999

ACCT. NO.	ACCOUNT TITLE	DEBITS	CREDITS

Name_____

SANCHEZ COMPANY
GENERAL JOURNAL

DATE (or entry no.)	ACCOUNT TITLES AND EXPLANATION	POST. REF.	DEBIT	CREDIT

Exercise 2-9   Name _____
                                         _____

Cash	Accounts Payable	Utilities Expense

	Notes Payable	Supplies Expense

Accounts Receivable	Capital Stock	Salaries Expense

Trucks	Service Revenue	

Exercise 2-10   **SANCHEZ COMPANY**

Trial Balance

March 31, 1999

ACCT. NO.	ACCOUNT TITLE	DEBITS	CREDITS

Exercise 2-11

_____
_____
_____
_____
_____
_____
_____
_____
_____
_____
_____
_____
_____

(in thousands)	Oct 1, 1995	Oct 2, 1994	Increase or (Decrease) 1995 over 1994		Percent of Total Assets (End of Fiscal Year)
			Dollars	Percent	

_____

GENERAL JOURNAL

DATE (or entry no.)	ACCOUNT TITLES AND EXPLANATION	POST. REF.	DEBIT	CREDIT

Name_____

_____

_____ , INC.

GENERAL JOURNAL   Page____

DATE (or entry no.)	ACCOUNT TITLES AND EXPLANATION	POST. REF.	DEBIT	CREDIT

Name _____

_____

_____ , INC.

GENERAL JOURNAL   Page ____

DATE (or entry no.)		ACCOUNT TITLES AND EXPLANATION	POST. REF.	DEBIT	CREDIT

GENERAL LEDGER

Cash   ACCOUNT NO. **100**

DATE	EXPLANATION	POST. REF.	DEBIT	CREDIT	BALANCE

Accounts Receivable   ACCOUNT NO. **103**

DATE	EXPLANATION	POST. REF.	DEBIT	CREDIT	BALANCE

Trucks   ACCOUNT NO. **150**

DATE	EXPLANATION	POST. REF.	DEBIT	CREDIT	BALANCE

Office Furniture   ACCOUNT NO. **160**

DATE	EXPLANATION	POST. REF.	DEBIT	CREDIT	BALANCE

Problem 2-3 or 2-3A (continued)
a. and c. (continued)

Name _____

_____

_____ ACCOUNT NO. _____

DATE	EXPLANATION	POST. REF.	DEBIT	CREDIT	BALANCE

_____ ACCOUNT NO. _____

DATE	EXPLANATION	POST. REF.	DEBIT	CREDIT	BALANCE

_____ ACCOUNT NO. _____

DATE	EXPLANATION	POST. REF.	DEBIT	CREDIT	BALANCE

_____ ACCOUNT NO. _____

DATE	EXPLANATION	POST. REF.	DEBIT	CREDIT	BALANCE

_____ ACCOUNT NO. _____

DATE	EXPLANATION	POST. REF.	DEBIT	CREDIT	BALANCE

_____ ACCOUNT NO. _____

DATE	EXPLANATION	POST. REF.	DEBIT	CREDIT	BALANCE

ACCOUNT NO. _____

DATE	EXPLANATION	POST. REF.	DEBIT	CREDIT	BALANCE

ACCOUNT NO. _____

DATE	EXPLANATION	POST. REF.	DEBIT	CREDIT	BALANCE

ACCOUNT NO. _____

DATE	EXPLANATION	POST. REF.	DEBIT	CREDIT	BALANCE

ACCOUNT NO. _____

DATE	EXPLANATION	POST. REF.	DEBIT	CREDIT	BALANCE

ACCOUNT NO. _____

DATE	EXPLANATION	POST. REF.	DEBIT	CREDIT	BALANCE

ACCOUNT NO. _____

DATE	EXPLANATION	POST. REF.	DEBIT	CREDIT	BALANCE

Problem 2-3 or 2-3A (concluded)

d.

Name _____

_____

_____

Trial Balance

_____ 31, 1999

ACCT. NO.	ACCOUNT TITLE	DEBITS	CREDITS

Trial Balance
December 31, 1999

ACCT. NO.	ACCOUNT TITLE	DEBITS	CREDITS

JACOBS CORPORATION
GENERAL JOURNAL

Page _____

DATE (or entry no.)	ACCOUNT TITLES AND EXPLANATION	POST. REF.	DEBIT	CREDIT

b.

JACOBS CORPORATION
T-Accounts

Cash	Service Revenue

Capital Stock	Advertising Expense

	Gas and Oil Expense

Dividends	Miscellaneous Expense

c.

JACOBS CORPORATION
Income Statement
For the Period Ended January 15 through April 15, 1999

		Percent of Total Assets		Increase or (Decrease) 1996 over 1995		December 31,	
		1995	1996	Percent	Dollars	1995	1996

Annual Report Analysis 2-2 (concluded)   Name_____

_____

Comments: _____

_____

_____

_____

_____

_____

_____

Annual Report Analysis 2-3

_____

_____

_____

_____

_____

_____

_____

_____

_____

_____

_____

_____

_____

_____

_____

_____

_____

_____

_____

_____

_____

_____

Ethics Case–Writing Experience 2-4

_____

_____

_____

_____

_____

_____

_____

_____

_____

_____

_____

_____

_____

_____

_____

_____

_____

_____

Exercise 3-1

1._____   2._____

Exercise 3-2

1._____   2._____

Exercise 3-3

1._____   2._____

Exercise 3-4

a.

b.

Exercise 3-5

Exercise 3-6

a.

b.

Exercise 3-7

Exercise 3-8

Exercise 3-9

Exercise 3-10

Exercise 3-11

Exercise 3-12

Exercise 3-13

Exercise 3-14

a. _____
_____
_____
_____

b. _____
_____
_____
_____

Exercise 3-15

	Effect on Net Income	Effect on Balance Sheet Items		
Failure to Recognize		Assets	Liabilities	Stockholders' Equity
1. Depreciation on a building.				
2. Consumption of supplies on hand.				
3. The earning of ticket revenue received in advance.				
4. The earning of interest on a bank account.				
5. Salaries incurred but unpaid.				

Exercise 3-16

_____, **INC.**
GENERAL JOURNAL

DATE (or entry no.)	ACCOUNT TITLES AND EXPLANATION	POST. REF.	DEBIT	CREDIT

GENERAL JOURNAL

DATE (or entry no.)	ACCOUNT TITLES AND EXPLANATION	POST. REF.	DEBIT	CREDIT

_____ COMPANY

Explanation of Corrections

	1999	2000
Reported net income		

a. _____

b. _____

a. _____
_____
_____
_____
_____
_____
_____
_____
_____
_____
_____
_____

b. _____**Exhibit A**_____

Approximate Income Statement for 1999

Annual Report Analysis 3-3

	Dollar Amount of Net Income	Percentage of 1986 Net Income
1986		
1987		
1988		
1989		
1990		
1991		
1992		
1993		
1994		
1995		
1996		

Exercise 4-1

_____
_____
_____
_____
_____
_____
_____
_____
_____
_____

Exercise 4-2

	Trial Balance		Income Statement		Statement of Retained Earnings		Balance Sheet	
	Debit	Credit	Debit	Credit	Debit	Credit	Debit	Credit
a. Accounts Receivable								
b. Accounts Payable								
c. Interest Revenue								
d. Advertising Expense								
e. Capital Stock								
f. Service Revenue								
g. Net income for the month								
h. Retained Earnings								

Exercise 4-3

	Statement of Retained Earnings		Balance Sheet	
	Debit	Credit	Debit	Credit

Exercise 4-4

	Statement of Retained Earnings		Balance Sheet	
	Debit	Credit	Debit	Credit

Exercise 4-5

_____
_____
_____
_____
_____
_____
_____

Name _____

_____

PRINTER REPAIR COMPANY
Work Sheet
For the Year Ended December 31, 1999

ACCOUNT TITLE	TRIAL BALANCE		ADJUSTMENTS		ADJUSTED TRIAL BALANCE		INCOME STATEMENT		STATEMENT OF RETAINED EARNINGS		BALANCE SHEET	
	DEBIT	CREDIT	DEBIT	CREDIT	DEBIT	CREDIT	DEBIT	CREDIT	DEBIT	CREDIT	DEBIT	CREDIT

TEXBAN CORPORATION
Statement of Retained Earnings
For the Year Ended December 31, 1999

Exercise 4-8

a.

b.

Exercise 4-9

PRINTER REPAIR COMPANY

DATE (or entry no.)	ACCOUNT TITLES AND EXPLANATION	POST. REF.	DEBIT	CREDIT
	Adjusting Entries			

PRINTER REPAIR COMPANY

DATE (or entry no.)		ACCOUNT TITLES AND EXPLANATION	POST. REF.	DEBIT	CREDIT	
		Closing Entries				

Exercise 4-10

Income Summary

Exercise 4-11   COLD STREAM CAMPGROUND

Rental Revenue   Dividends

Salaries Expense   Income Summary

Depreciation Expense–Buildings

Utilities Expense   Retained Earnings

Exercise 4-12

Name _____

DATE (or entry no.)		ACCOUNT TITLES AND EXPLANATION	POST. REF.	DEBIT	CREDIT
		Closing Entries			

Exercise 4-13

_____
_____
_____
_____
_____
_____
_____
_____

Exercise 4-14

a. _____ b. _____ c. _____ d. _____ e. _____

f. _____ g. _____ h. _____ i. _____ j. _____

Exercise 4-15

_____
_____
_____
_____
_____
_____
_____
_____
_____

Name_____

_____

_____ COMPANY
GENERAL JOURNAL

DATE (or entry no.)		ACCOUNT TITLES AND EXPLANATION	POST. REF.	DEBIT	CREDIT
		Closing Entries			

a.　　　　　　　　_____ **, INC.**

Income Statement

For the Year Ended December 31, 1999

b.　　　　　　　　_____ **, INC.**

Statement of Retained Earnings

For the Year Ended December 31, 1999

Name_____

_____

_____, **INC.**

_____

Balance Sheet

December 31,1999

Assets															

Liabilities and Stockholders' Equity															

Problem 4-2 or 4-2A (continued)
d.

Name_____

_____

GENERAL JOURNAL

DATE (or entry no.)		ACCOUNT TITLES AND EXPLANATION	POST. REF.	DEBIT	CREDIT
		Closing Entries			

Chapter 4

Problem 4-2 or 4-2A (concluded)

e.

Name_____

_____ , INC.

Post-Closing Trial Balance

December 31, 1999

	ACCOUNT TITLE	DEBITS	CREDITS

Problem 4-3 or 4-3A

Work Sheet for Part A of this problem appears in the back of this manual.

Name_____

_____

_____ COMPANY

GENERAL JOURNAL

DATE (or entry no.)		ACCOUNT TITLES AND EXPLANATION	POST. REF.	DEBIT	CREDIT
b.		**Adjusting Entries**			

Problem 4-3 or 4-3A (concluded)
c.

Name_____

_____

_____ **COMPANY**
GENERAL JOURNAL

DATE (or entry no.)		ACCOUNT TITLES AND EXPLANATION	POST. REF.	DEBIT	CREDIT
		Closing Entries			

_____ **COMPANY**
GENERAL JOURNAL

DATE (or entry no.)		ACCOUNT TITLES AND EXPLANATION	POST. REF.	DEBIT	CREDIT
b.		**Closing Entries**			

HEATHER AND DAN HOLT

Income Statement

For the Year Ended December 31, 1999

Annual Report Analysis 4-2

	1996	1995

Annual Report Analysis 4-2 (concluded)   Name_____

_____
_____
_____
_____
_____
_____
_____
_____
_____
_____
_____
_____
_____
_____
_____
_____
_____
_____
_____
_____
_____
_____
_____
_____
_____
_____
_____
_____
_____
_____
_____

Broader Perspective–Writing Experience 4-3

_____
_____
_____
_____
_____
_____
_____
_____
_____
_____
_____
_____

Exercise 5-1

1._____   2._____   3._____   4._____   5._____
6._____   7._____   8._____   9._____   10._____

Exercise 5-2

a.

b.

Exercise 5-3

Exercise 5-4

a.

b.

c.

Exercise 5-5

a.

b.

Exercise 5-6

1.
2.
3.
4.
5.
6.
7.
8.
9.
10.
11.
12.
13.
14.

1. _____

2. _____

3. _____

4. _____

5. _____

a.

b.

Name _____

_____ **COMPANY**

a.

b.

LING CLOTHING COMPANY

a.
_____
_____
_____
_____

b.
_____
_____
_____
_____

c.
_____
_____
_____
_____
_____
_____
_____
_____
_____
_____
_____
_____
_____
_____
_____
_____
_____
_____
_____
_____

Exercise 6-1

Title of Account	Increase by (debit or credit)	Decrease by (debit or credit)	Normal Balance (debit or credit)
Merchandise Inventory			
Sales			
Sales Returns and Allowances			
Sales Discounts			
Accounts Receivable			
Purchases			
Purchase Returns and Allowances			
Purchase Discounts			
Accounts Payable			
Transportation-In			

Exercise 6-2

a.

SILVER COMPANY

DATE (or entry no.)	ACCOUNT TITLES AND EXPLANATION	POST. REF.	DEBIT	CREDIT

MILTON COMPANY

DATE (or entry no.)	ACCOUNT TITLES AND EXPLANATION	POST. REF.	DEBIT	CREDIT

b.

SILVER COMPANY

DATE (or entry no.)	ACCOUNT TITLES AND EXPLANATION	POST. REF.	DEBIT	CREDIT

MILTON COMPANY

DATE (or entry no.)	ACCOUNT TITLES AND EXPLANATION	POST. REF.	DEBIT	CREDIT

Chapter 6

Exercise 6-3

Buyer's Books

DATE (or entry no.)		ACCOUNT TITLES AND EXPLANATION	POST. REF.	DEBIT	CREDIT

Seller's Books

DATE (or entry no.)		ACCOUNT TITLES AND EXPLANATION	POST. REF.	DEBIT	CREDIT

Exercise 6-4

Exercise 6-5

	Gross Selling Price	Cash Paid
a.		
b.		
c.		
d.		

Exercise 6-6

	Cash Discount Available	Amount of Cash Paid
a.		
b.		
c.		
d.		

Exercise 6-7

DATE (or entry no.)	ACCOUNT TITLES AND EXPLANATION	POST. REF.	DEBIT	CREDIT
a.				
b.				

Exercise 6-8

Exercise 6-9

Case 1:

Exercise 6-9 (concluded)

Case 2:

Case 3:

Exercise 6-10

a.

b.

c.

d.

e.

Exercise 6-11 appears on the following page.

Exercise 6-12

ACCOUNT TITLES	TRIAL BALANCE		ADJUSTMENTS		ADJUSTED TRIAL BALANCE		INCOME STATEMENT		BALANCE SHEET	
	DEBIT	CREDIT	DEBIT	CREDIT	DEBIT	CREDIT	DEBIT	CREDIT	DEBIT	CREDIT

Problem 6-1 or 6-1A
a.

Name_____

_____ **COMPANY**
GENERAL JOURNAL

DATE (or entry no.)	ACCOUNT TITLES AND EXPLANATION	POST. REF.	DEBIT	CREDIT

_____ **COMPANY**

GENERAL JOURNAL

DATE (or entry no.)		ACCOUNT TITLES AND EXPLANATION	POST. REF.	DEBIT	CREDIT

Problem 6-4 or 6-4A
a.

Name_____

_____

_____ **COMPANY**
GENERAL JOURNAL   **Page____**

DATE (or entry no.)	ACCOUNT TITLES AND EXPLANATION	POST. REF.	DEBIT	CREDIT

_____ **COMPANY**
GENERAL JOURNAL   Page ____

DATE (or entry no.)	ACCOUNT TITLES AND EXPLANATION	POST. REF.	DEBIT	CREDIT

Name_____

_____

_____ **COMPANY**

GENERAL LEDGER

Cash   ACCOUNT NO. **100**

DATE		EXPLANATION	POST. REF.	DEBIT	CREDIT	BALANCE

Accounts Receivable   ACCOUNT NO. **103**

DATE		EXPLANATION	POST. REF.	DEBIT	CREDIT	BALANCE

_____   ACCOUNT NO. _____

DATE		EXPLANATION	POST. REF.	DEBIT	CREDIT	BALANCE

_____   ACCOUNT NO. _____

DATE		EXPLANATION	POST. REF.	DEBIT	CREDIT	BALANCE

ACCOUNT NO. _____

DATE		EXPLANATION	POST. REF.	DEBIT	CREDIT	BALANCE

ACCOUNT NO. _____

DATE		EXPLANATION	POST. REF.	DEBIT	CREDIT	BALANCE

ACCOUNT NO. _____

DATE		EXPLANATION	POST. REF.	DEBIT	CREDIT	BALANCE

ACCOUNT NO. _____

DATE		EXPLANATION	POST. REF.	DEBIT	CREDIT	BALANCE

ACCOUNT NO. _____

DATE		EXPLANATION	POST. REF.	DEBIT	CREDIT	BALANCE

ACCOUNT NO. _____

DATE		EXPLANATION	POST. REF.	DEBIT	CREDIT	BALANCE

Name _____

ACCOUNT NO. _____

DATE		EXPLANATION	POST. REF.	DEBIT	CREDIT	BALANCE	

ACCOUNT NO. _____

DATE		EXPLANATION	POST. REF.	DEBIT	CREDIT	BALANCE	

ACCOUNT NO. _____

DATE		EXPLANATION	POST. REF.	DEBIT	CREDIT	BALANCE	

ACCOUNT NO. _____

DATE		EXPLANATION	POST. REF.	DEBIT	CREDIT	BALANCE	

ACCOUNT NO. _____

DATE		EXPLANATION	POST. REF.	DEBIT	CREDIT	BALANCE	

ACCOUNT NO. _____

DATE		EXPLANATION	POST. REF.	DEBIT	CREDIT	BALANCE	

Name_____

_____ **COMPANY**

Trial Balance

May 31, 1999

ACCT. NO.	ACCOUNT TITLE	DEBITS	CREDITS

Problem 6-4 or 6-4A (continued)
d.

Name _____

_____ **COMPANY**

Income Statement

For the Month Ended May 31,1999

THE WESTERN WEAR COMPANY

Balance Sheet

May 31,1999

Assets

Liabilities and Stockholders' Equity

Problem 6-5 or 6-5A
Work Sheet for Part A of this problem appears in the back of this manual.
b.

_____ **COMPANY**
Income Statement
For the Year Ended December 31,1999

c.   _____ **COMPANY**

Statement of Retained Earnings

For the Year Ended December 31, 1999

d.   _____ **COMPANY**

Balance Sheet

December 31,1999

_____ **COMPANY**
GENERAL JOURNAL

DATE (or entry no.)		ACCOUNT TITLES AND EXPLANATION	POST. REF.	DEBIT	CREDIT
		Closing Entries			

Name_____

_____

CANDY'S SHIRTS, INC.

Income Statements

For the Years Ended December 31, 1998 and 1999

	1998	1999

b.

CANDY'S SHIRTS, INC.

Cash Inflows and Outflows

	1998	1999

Business Decision Case 6-2

	1996	1995	1994

Annual Report Analysis 6-3   Name _____

_____
_____
_____
_____
_____
_____
_____
_____
_____
_____
_____
_____
_____
_____
_____
_____
_____
_____
_____
_____
_____
_____
_____
_____

Ethics Case–Writing Experience 6-4

a. _____
_____
_____

b. _____
_____
_____

c. _____
_____
_____
_____
_____
_____
_____
_____

Exercise 7-1

CROCKER COMPANY

Schedule of Corrected Net Income

Year	1997	1998	1999	Total

Exercise 7-2

_____
_____
_____
_____

Work Sheets for Exercises 7-3, 7-4, and 7-5 appear on the following pages.

Exercise 7-6

a.   **KETTLE COMPANY**

FIFO	LIFO	Weighted Average

b. _____
_____
_____

Exercise 7-7

CUSTER COMPANY
GENERAL JOURNAL

DATE (or entry no.)	ACCOUNT TITLES AND EXPLANATION	POST. REF.	DEBIT	CREDIT

Exercise 7-3

MIAMI DISCOUNT COMPANY

Date	Purchased			Sold			Balance		
	Units	Unit Cost	Total Cost	Units	Unit Cost	Total Cost	Units	Unit Cost	Total Cost

Exercise 7-4

MIAMI DISCOUNT COMPANY

Date	Purchased			Sold			Balance		
	Units	Unit Cost	Total Cost	Units	Unit Cost	Total Cost	Units	Unit Cost	Total Cost

Name_____

LONDON COMPANY

Date	Purchased			Sold			Balance		
	Units	Unit Cost	Total Cost	Units	Unit Cost	Total Cost	Units	Unit Cost	Total Cost

GAMBLE COMPANY
GENERAL JOURNAL

DATE (or entry no.)	ACCOUNT TITLES AND EXPLANATION	POST. REF.	DEBIT	CREDIT

WELLS COMPANY
GENERAL JOURNAL

DATE (or entry no.)	ACCOUNT TITLES AND EXPLANATION	POST. REF.	DEBIT	CREDIT

Exercise 7-10
_____
_____
_____
_____
_____
_____

Exercise 7-11
_____
_____
_____
_____

Exercise 7-12
_____
_____
_____

Exercise 7-13

Exercise 7-14

Exercise 7-15

Item	Cost	Market	Lower of Cost or Market

Exercise 7-16

Items	Cost	Market

Exercise 7-17

Exercise 7-18

Exercise 7-19

	Cost		Retail	

Problem 7-1 or 7-1A

Name_____

_____ **COMPANY**

Schedule of Corrected Income

	1998	1999	2000	Total

Name _____

a. _____ **COMPANY**

	1995	1996	1997	1998	Total

b.

c.

_____ **COMPANY** _____

a.

b.

c.

Name

CORAL COMPANY

a.

b.

c.

THIMBLE COMPANY
GENERAL JOURNAL

DATE (or entry no.)	ACCOUNT TITLES AND EXPLANATION	POST. REF.	DEBIT	CREDIT

Problem 7-6 or 7-6A

a.

Name_____

_____ COMPANY
GENERAL JOURNAL

DATE (or entry no.)	ACCOUNT TITLES AND EXPLANATION	POST. REF.	DEBIT	CREDIT

Name_____

_____

_____ **COMPANY**

GENERAL JOURNAL

DATE (or entry no.)	ACCOUNT TITLES AND EXPLANATION	POST. REF.	DEBIT	CREDIT

Problem 7-7 or 7-7A

a. (1) FIFO–perpetual:

_____ COMPANY

Schedule of Alternative Inventory Valuations

Date	Purchased			Sold			Balance		
	Units	Unit Cost	Total Cost	Units	Unit Cost	Total Cost	Units	Unit Cost	Total Cost

Problem 7-7 or 7-7A (continued)
a. (2) LIFO–perpetual:

_____ **COMPANY**

Schedule of Alternative Inventory Valuations

Date	Purchased			Sold			Balance		
	Units	Unit Cost	Total Cost	Units	Unit Cost	Total Cost	Units	Unit Cost	Total Cost

Problem 7-7 or 7-7A (continued)
a. (2) (concluded)

Name _____

_____ COMPANY

Schedule of Alternative Inventory Valuations

Date	Purchased			Sold			Balance		
	Units	Unit Cost	Total Cost	Units	Unit Cost	Total Cost	Units	Unit Cost	Total Cost

Chapter 7

Problem 7-7 or 7-7A (continued)

a. (3) Weighted-average–perpetual (moving average):

Name _____

_____ COMPANY

Schedule of Alternative Inventory Valuations

Date	Purchased			Sold			Balance		
	Units	Unit Cost	Total Cost	Units	Unit Cost	Total Cost	Units	Unit Cost	Total Cost

Problem 7-7 (concluded)
b.

Name _____

_____

	Units	Unit Cost	Total Cost	
(1) FIFO–periodic				
(2) LIFO–periodic:				
(3) Weighted-average–periodic:				

Problem 7-7A (concluded)
b.

BRAXTON COMPANY

Schedule of Alternative Inventory Valuations

Periodic Procedures

	Units	Unit Cost	Total Cost
(1) Cost of goods available for sale:			
(2) Cost of goods available for sale:			
(3) Weighted-average unit cost:			

Name _____

_____ **COMPANY**

Computation of Gross Margin

a.

b.

c.

_____ **COMPANY**

Computation of Gross Margin

d.

Problem 7-9 or 7-9A

Name _____

_____ **COMPANY**

Schedule of Inventory Valuation

December 31, 1998

Item	Cost	Market	Lower of Cost or Market

a.   **LIVELY COMPANY**

b.

Computation of Ending Merchandise Inventory

Name_____

_____

a.   **BRAZOS COMPANY**

_____

_____

_____

_____

_____

_____

b.   **BRAZOS COMPANY**
Income Statement for the Quarters Ended March 31, 1998, and June 30, 1998,
and for the Six Months Ended June 30, 1998

	First Quarter	Second Quarter	Six Months Ended 6/30/98

Problem 7-11 or 7-11A   Name_____

_____ **COMPANY**

	Cost	Retail

Name _____

_____

a.   **Green**   **Lewis**

_____   _____

_____   _____

_____   _____

_____   _____

_____   _____

_____   _____

_____   _____

_____   _____

_____   _____

_____   _____

_____   _____

_____   _____

_____   _____

_____   _____

b. _____

_____

_____

_____

_____

_____

_____

_____

_____

_____

_____

_____

_____

_____

c.   **Green**   **Lewis**

_____   _____

_____   _____

_____   _____

_____   _____

_____   _____

_____   _____

_____   _____

_____   _____

_____   _____

_____   _____

CONNIE DALTON

Annual Report Analysis 7-3

Exercise 8-1

a. _____ b. _____ c. _____ d. _____

e. _____ f. _____ g. _____ h. _____

Exercise 8-2

Exercise 8-3

Exercise 8-4

REED COMPANY

Bank Reconciliation

October 31, 1999

Exercise 8-5

Exercise 8-6

Exercise 8-7

Exercise 8-8

HOLDER COMPANY

Bank Reconciliation

October 31, 19–

Exercise 8-9

Exercise 8-10

Exercise 8-11

ENGLAND COMPANY
Bank Reconciliation
June 30, 1999

Entry

	DEBIT	CREDIT

TIFFANY COMPANY
Bank Reconciliation
July 31,1999

Entry

	DEBIT	CREDIT

a.

IRISH COMPANY

Bank Reconciliation

July 31, 1999

b.   **Entry**

	DEBIT	CREDIT

a.

HUGHES COMPANY

Bank Reconciliation

May 31, 1999

b.   **Entry**

	DEBIT	CREDIT

Name_____

_____

_____ **COMPANY**

GENERAL JOURNAL

DATE (or entry no.)	ACCOUNT TITLES AND EXPLANATION	POST. REF.	DEBIT	CREDIT

Chapter 8

Problem 8-4 or 8-4A

Name_____

_____

_____ **COMPANY**

GENERAL JOURNAL

DATE (or entry no.)	ACCOUNT TITLES AND EXPLANATION	POST. REF.	DEBIT	CREDIT

Business Decision Case 8-1   Name _____

_____

Business Decision Case 8-2

a.

b.   Bank Reconciliation
                           December 31, 1999

c.

Annual Report Analysis 8-4   Name _____

_____

_____
_____
_____
_____
_____
_____
_____
_____
_____
_____
_____
_____
_____

Annual Report Analysis 8-5

	1996	1995

_____
_____
_____
_____
_____
_____

Ethics Case–Writing Experience 8-6

_____
_____
_____
_____
_____
_____
_____
_____
_____
_____
_____
_____

Exercise 9-1

a.

b.

Exercise 9-2

Exercise 9-3

Exercise 9-4

Exercise 9-5

Exercise 9-6

Exercise 9-7

Exercise 9-8

Crawford, Inc.		Dunston, Inc.	

Exercise 9-9

Crawford, Inc.		Dunston, Inc.	

Name _____

Exercise 9-10

a.

b.

Exercise 9-11

a.

b.

Exercise 9-12

GENERAL JOURNAL

DATE (or entry no.)		ACCOUNT TITLES AND EXPLANATION	POST. REF.	DEBIT	CREDIT
a.					
b.					

_____ **RESTAURANT**
GENERAL JOURNAL

DATE (or entry no.)	ACCOUNT TITLES AND EXPLANATION	POST. REF.	DEBIT	CREDIT

GENERAL JOURNAL

DATE (or entry no.)		ACCOUNT TITLES AND EXPLANATION	POST. REF.	DEBIT	CREDIT
a.					
b.					

Problem 9-4 or 9-4A

Name _____

_____

a.
_____
_____
_____
_____
_____
_____
_____
_____
_____
_____
_____
_____
_____
_____
_____
_____
_____
_____
_____
_____

GENERAL JOURNAL

DATE (or entry no.)	ACCOUNT TITLES AND EXPLANATION	POST. REF.	DEBIT	CREDIT
b.				
c.				

Problem 9-5 or 9-5A   Name_____

_____

GENERAL JOURNAL

DATE (or entry no.)	ACCOUNT TITLES AND EXPLANATION	POST. REF.	DEBIT	CREDIT

Name_____

_____

GENERAL JOURNAL

DATE (or entry no.)	ACCOUNT TITLES AND EXPLANATION	POST. REF.	DEBIT	CREDIT

_____ , INC.

GENERAL JOURNAL

DATE (or entry no.)	ACCOUNT TITLES AND EXPLANATION	POST. REF.	DEBIT	CREDIT

Business Decision Case 9-1

a.

b.

Business Decision Case 9-2

Company	Net Sales	Average Net Accounts Receivable	Accounts Receivable Turnover

Company	Days in Year (365)	Accounts Receivable Turnover	No. of Days' Sales in Accts. Receivable

Exercise 10-1

Exercise 10-2

	Land		Building	

Exercise 10-3

Exercise 10-4

Exercise 10-5

Exercise 10-6

a. Straight-line:

b. Units-of-production:

c. Sum-of-the-years'-digits:

d. Double-declining-balance:

Exercise 10-7

Exercise 10-8

a.

b.

Exercise 10-9

	Depreciation Expense	Accumulated Depreciation	Book Value

Exercise 10-10

Exercise 10-11

Exercise 10-12

Exercise 10-13

Exercise 10-14

Exercise 10-15

Effect on Net Income	1998	1999	2000	2001	2002

_____ **COMPANY**
Schedule of Machine Cost

Name _____

MAXWELL COMPANY

Schedule of Land Cost

PRESSLER COMPANY
Schedule of Costs of Assets Acquired

DAWSON TOWING COMPANY
Schedule of Truck Cost

a.

b.

c.

Name_____

_____

TIMOTHY COMPANY
GENERAL JOURNAL

DATE (or entry no.)	ACCOUNT TITLES AND EXPLANATION	POST. REF.	DEBIT	CREDIT
a.				
b.				
c.				

Problem 10-4
a.

Name_____

JAYSON COMPANY
Schedule of Costs Incurred

Item	Land	Land Improvements	Building	Machinery

Name _____

JAYSON COMPANY
GENERAL JOURNAL

DATE (or entry no.)	ACCOUNT TITLES AND EXPLANATION	POST. REF.	DEBIT	CREDIT

Name _____

_____

PEACH COMPANY

Schedule of Building Cost

December 31, 1999

PEACH COMPANY
GENERAL JOURNAL

DATE (or entry no.)	ACCOUNT TITLES AND EXPLANATION	POST. REF.	DEBIT	CREDIT

Name_____

LAND COMPANY
GENERAL JOURNAL

Page _____

DATE (or entry no.)	ACCOUNT TITLES AND EXPLANATION	POST. REF.	DEBIT	CREDIT
a.				
b.				
c.				
d.				

Chapter 10

CARDINE COMPANY

a. Straight-line depreciation:

b. Units-of-production depreciation:

c. Sum-of-the-years'-digits depreciation:

d. Double-declining-balance depreciation:

Problem 10-6 or 10-6A   Name_____

_____ **COMPANY**

Year	Computations	Depreciation Expense	
		1998	1999
a.	**Straight-line:**		
b.	**Sum-of-the-years'-digits:**		
c.	**Double-declining-balance:**		

CRAY COMPANY
Schedule to Compute Cost of Land, Buildings, and Land Improvements
December 31, 1998

a.	Land	Buildings	Land Improvements
Debits			
Credits			
b.			

c.   **CRAY COMPANY**
                                                GENERAL JOURNAL

DATE (or entry no.)		ACCOUNT TITLES AND EXPLANATION	POST. REF.	DEBIT	CREDIT

d. _____

_____

_____

_____

_____

_____

_____

_____

_____

a.   **BESLER COMPANY**

b.

Business Decision Case 10-3

Year	Name of Company	Net Operating Income (in millions)	Operating Assets (in millions)	Rate of Return on Operating Assets

Annual Report Analysis 10-5

a.

b.

Exercise 11-1

a.

b.

Exercise 11-2

Exercise 11-3

a.

b.

Exercise 11-4

Exercise 11-5

a.

b.

c.

d.

e.

Exercise 11-6

Exercise 11-7

Exercise 11-8

Exercise 11-9

Exercise 11-10

Exercise 11-11

Exercise 11-12

Journal entry:

GENERAL JOURNAL

DATE (or entry no.)	ACCOUNT TITLES AND EXPLANATION	POST. REF.	DEBIT	CREDIT

Problem 11-2 or 11-2A   Name _____

a. _____**COMPANY**

Schedule to Compute Book Value

December 31, 1998

_____**COMPANY**

GENERAL JOURNAL

DATE (or entry no.)	ACCOUNT TITLES AND EXPLANATION	POST. REF.	DEBIT	CREDIT
b.				
c.				

_____ **COMPANY**
GENERAL JOURNAL

DATE (or entry no.)	ACCOUNT TITLES AND EXPLANATION	POST. REF.	DEBIT	CREDIT

Name_____

_____

_____ **COMPANY**

GENERAL JOURNAL

DATE (or entry no.)		ACCOUNT TITLES AND EXPLANATION	POST. REF.	DEBIT	CREDIT

_____ **COMPANY**
GENERAL JOURNAL

DATE (or entry no.)	ACCOUNT TITLES AND EXPLANATION	POST. REF.	DEBIT	CREDIT

_____ **COMPANY**
GENERAL JOURNAL

DATE (or entry no.)	ACCOUNT TITLES AND EXPLANATION	POST. REF.	DEBIT	CREDIT

BROWN COMPANY
GENERAL JOURNAL   **Page** ____

DATE (or entry no.)		ACCOUNT TITLES AND EXPLANATION	POST. REF.	DEBIT	CREDIT

YORK MINING COMPANY

a.

b.

c.

_____ **COMPANY**

GENERAL JOURNAL

DATE (or entry no.)	ACCOUNT TITLES AND EXPLANATION	POST. REF.	DEBIT	CREDIT

_____ **COMPANY**
GENERAL JOURNAL

DATE (or entry no.)	ACCOUNT TITLES AND EXPLANATION	POST. REF.	DEBIT	CREDIT

SHIRLEY COMPANY
GENERAL JOURNAL

DATE (or entry no.)		ACCOUNT TITLES AND EXPLANATION	POST. REF.	DEBIT	CREDIT
a.					
b.					

Business Decision Case 11-1 (continued)
c.

Name_____

_____

SHIRLEY COMPANY
GENERAL JOURNAL

DATE (or entry no.)	ACCOUNT TITLES AND EXPLANATION	POST. REF.	DEBIT	CREDIT

d.

e.

TYRE, INC.
GENERAL JOURNAL

DATE (or entry no.)	ACCOUNT TITLES AND EXPLANATION	POST. REF.	DEBIT	CREDIT

b.

_____
_____
_____
_____
_____
_____
_____
_____
_____

Annual Report Analysis 11-3

Name _____
_____

_____

_____

_____

_____

_____

_____

_____

_____

_____

_____

_____

_____

_____

_____

_____

_____

_____

_____

_____

_____

_____

_____

_____

_____

Ethics Case–Writing Experience 11-4

a. _____

_____

_____

_____

_____

b. _____

_____

_____

_____

_____

c. _____

_____

_____

_____

_____

_____

Exercise 12-1

Exercise 12-2

Exercise 12-3

Exercise 12-4

Exercise 12-5

Exercise 12-6

Exercise 12-7

Exercise 12-8

Dividends to Each Class of Stock

Year	Dividends to	Assumptions	
		A	B

Name_____

_____

_____ **COMPANY**

GENERAL JOURNAL

DATE (or entry no.)	ACCOUNT TITLES AND EXPLANATION	POST. REF.	DEBIT	CREDIT

_____COMPANY

Balance Sheet

March 1, 1998

Assets							

Problem 12-3 or 12-3A
a.

Name _____

_____**COMPANY**

Cash

_____**COMPANY**
Balance Sheet
July ___, 1998

Assets

Common Stock	Paid-In Capital in Excess of Stated Value–Common

Stockholders' equity:

c.

Common Stock

Stockholders' equity:

Problem 12-4 or 12-4A

a.

Name_____

_____

_____ **COMPANY**

GENERAL JOURNAL

DATE (or entry no.)	ACCOUNT TITLES AND EXPLANATION	POST. REF.	DEBIT	CREDIT

b.

_____**COMPANY**

Partial Balance Sheet

_____ ____, 1998

c. (Problem 12-4 only)

_____**COMPANY**

Partial Balance Sheet

December 31, 1998

a.

Stockholders' equity:

b. Computation of book values:

c.

Computation of Book Values–Preferred and Common
As of December 31, 1998

Name _____

_____

a. _____   Computation of Dividends per Share _____

_____

Rudd Company:

Clay Company:

b. _____

c. _____

a.   Computation of Book Values

West Corporation:

East Corporation:

b.

Name _____

_____

_____
_____
_____
_____

Year	Name of Company	Net Income (in thousands)	Average Common S/H Equity (in thousands)	Ratio of Net Income to Average S/H Equity

_____
_____
_____
_____
_____
_____
_____

Ethics Case–Writing Experience 12-4

a. _____
_____
_____
_____
_____
_____

b. _____
_____
_____
_____
_____
_____

c. _____
_____
_____
_____

YAMEY CORPORATION
Partial Balance Sheet
December 31, 1998

Exercise 13-2

Exercise 13-3

Exercise 13-4

a.

b.

Exercise 13-5

a.

b.

Exercise 13-6

a.

b.

Exercise 13-7

a.

b.

c.

Exercise 13-8

Exercise 13-9

a.

VISTA COMPANY

Income Statement

b.

VISTA COMPANY

Statement of Retained Earnings

Name_____

Exercise 13-10

CONNER COMPANY
Statement of Retained Earnings
For the Year Ended December 31, 1998

Exercise 13-11

PERRY CORPORATION
Calculation of Earnings per Share
December 31, 1998

Exercise 13-12
a.

DEAN COMPANY
Calculation of Earnings per Share
1999 and 1998

	1999	1996

b.

Partial Balance Sheet
December 31, 1998

Stockholders' equity:

Name_____

_____ **COMPANY**

GENERAL JOURNAL

DATE (or entry no.)		ACCOUNT TITLES AND EXPLANATION	POST. REF.	DEBIT	CREDIT

GENERAL JOURNAL

DATE (or entry no.)	ACCOUNT TITLES AND EXPLANATION	POST. REF.	DEBIT	CREDIT

TAYLOR CORPORATION
GENERAL JOURNAL

DATE (or entry no.)		ACCOUNT TITLES AND EXPLANATION	POST. REF.	DEBIT	CREDIT

KANE CORPORATION
Statement of Retained Earnings
For the Year Ended December 31, 1998

DAHL CORPORATION

Statement of Retained Earnings

For the Year Ended December 31, 1998

SAYERS COMPANY
GENERAL JOURNAL

DATE (or entry no.)		ACCOUNT TITLES AND EXPLANATION	POST. REF.	DEBIT	CREDIT

Problem 13-6 or 13-6A
a.

Name_____

_____

_____ **COMPANY**

GENERAL JOURNAL

DATE (or entry no.)	ACCOUNT TITLES AND EXPLANATION	POST. REF.	DEBIT	CREDIT

Name_____

_____

_____ **COMPANY**

Partial Balance Sheet

December 31, 1998

Problem 13-7 or 13-7A

a.

Name_____

_____

_____ **COMPANY**

GENERAL JOURNAL

DATE (or entry no.)	ACCOUNT TITLES AND EXPLANATION	POST. REF.	DEBIT	CREDIT

_____ **COMPANY**
GENERAL JOURNAL

DATE (or entry no.)	ACCOUNT TITLES AND EXPLANATION	POST. REF.	DEBIT	CREDIT

_____ **COMPANY**

Statement of Retained Earnings

For the Year Ended _____ 31, 1998

Name_____

_____

_____**COMPANY**

Partial Balance Sheet

_____ 31, 1998

_____ **COMPANY**

Income Statement

For the Year Ended December 31, 1998

_____ COMPANY
Statement of Retained Earnings
For the Year Ended December 31, 1998

a.

b.

c.

KEEL CORPORATION
GENERAL JOURNAL

DATE (or entry no.)	ACCOUNT TITLES AND EXPLANATION	POST. REF.	DEBIT	CREDIT

a.

	1996	1995

b.

c.

Ethics Case–Writing Experience

a.

b.

c.

Exercise 14-1

Exercise 14-2

Exercise 14-3

a.

b.

c.

Exercise 14-4

Exercise 14-5

a.

b.

Exercise 14-6

a.

b.

c.

Exercise 14-7

a.

b.

Exercise 14-8

a.

b.

c.

Exercise 14-9

a.

b.

c.

Exercise 14-10

a.

b.

Problem 14-1 or 14-1A

a.

Name_____

_____

_____ COMPANY
GENERAL JOURNAL

DATE (or entry no.)	ACCOUNT TITLES AND EXPLANATION	POST. REF.	DEBIT	CREDIT
b.				

Problem 14-2 or 14-2A
a.

Name _____

_____

_____

GENERAL JOURNAL

DATE (or entry no.)	ACCOUNT TITLES AND EXPLANATION	POST. REF.	DEBIT	CREDIT

b.

c.

GENERAL JOURNAL

DATE (or entry no.)	ACCOUNT TITLES AND EXPLANATION	POST. REF.	DEBIT	CREDIT

Problem 14-3 or 14-3A

a.

Name_____

_____

_____ COMPANY

GENERAL JOURNAL

DATE (or entry no.)		ACCOUNT TITLES AND EXPLANATION	POST. REF.	DEBIT	CREDIT
b.					

Name_____

_____ COMPANY
GENERAL JOURNAL   Page ____

DATE (or entry no.)	ACCOUNT TITLES AND EXPLANATION	POST. REF.	DEBIT	CREDIT

_____ **COMPANY**
Investment Account Balance
December 31, 2001

COMPANY AND SUBSIDIARY _____ **COMPANY**

Work Sheet for Consolidated Balance Sheet

January 2, 1999

	Company	Company	Eliminations Debit	Eliminations Credit	Consolidated Amounts
Assets					
Liabilities and Stockholders' Equity					

a.

_____**COMPANY AND SUBSIDIARY** _____ **COMPANY**

Consolidated Balance Sheet

January 2, 1999

Assets

Liabilities and Stockholders' Equity

COMPANY AND SUBSIDIARY _____ **COMPANY**

Work Sheet for Consolidated Financial Statements

December 31, 1999

	Company	Company	Eliminations Debit	Eliminations Credit	Consolidated Amounts

Income Statement

Statement of Retained Earnings

Dividends:

COMPANY AND SUBSIDIARY _____ COMPANY

Work Sheet for Consolidated Financial Statements
December 31, 1999

Balance Sheet	Company	Company	Eliminations Debit	Eliminations Credit	Consolidated Amounts
Assets					
Liabilities and Stockholders' Equity					

a.

Name _____

_____

_____**COMPANY AND SUBSIDIARY**_____**COMPANY**

Consolidated Income Statement

For the Year Ended December 31, 1999

b. _____**COMPANY AND SUBSIDIARY**_____**COMPANY**

Consolidated Statement of Retained Earnings

For the Year Ended December 31, 1999

Problem 14-7 or 14-7A (concluded)
b. (concluded)

_____**COMPANY AND SUBSIDIARY** _____**COMPANY**

Consolidated Balance Sheet

December 31, 1999

Assets

Liabilities and Stockholders' Equity

a.

_____

_____

_____

_____

_____

_____

_____

_____

_____

_____

_____

_____

_____

b.

BROWN COMPANY AND SUBSIDIARY COBB CORPORATION
Consolidated Balance Sheet
January 2, 1999

Assets

Liabilities and Stockholders' Equity

Exercise 15-1

DATE (or entry no.)		ACCOUNT TITLES AND EXPLANATION	POST. REF.	DEBIT	CREDIT

Exercise 15-2

a.

b.

c.

Exercise 15-3

Exercise 15-4

DATE (or entry no.)		ACCOUNT TITLES AND EXPLANATION	POST. REF.	DEBIT	CREDIT

Exercise 15-5

DATE (or entry no.)		ACCOUNT TITLES AND EXPLANATION	POST. REF.	DEBIT	CREDIT

Exercise 15-6

DATE (or entry no.)		ACCOUNT TITLES AND EXPLANATION	POST. REF.	DEBIT	CREDIT

Exercise 15-7

DATE (or entry no.)		ACCOUNT TITLES AND EXPLANATION	POST. REF.	DEBIT	CREDIT

Exercise 15-8

DATE (or entry no.)		ACCOUNT TITLES AND EXPLANATION	POST. REF.	DEBIT	CREDIT

Exercise 15-9

Exercise 15-10

Exercise 15-11

Exercise 15-12

a.

b.

c.

Exercise 15-13

GENERAL JOURNAL

DATE (or entry no.)	ACCOUNT TITLES AND EXPLANATION	POST. REF.	DEBIT	CREDIT

Problem 15-2 or 15-2A

Name _____

a.

b.

_____ **COMPANY**
GENERAL JOURNAL

DATE (or entry no.)	ACCOUNT TITLES AND EXPLANATION	POST. REF.	DEBIT	CREDIT

Problem 15-4

Name _____

a.   **CREATIVE WEB PAGE COMPANY**

b.   Discount Amortization Schedule

(A)	(B)	(C)	(D)	(E)
Interest	Bond Interest	Cash Credit	Discount on Bonds	Carrying Value
Payment Date	Expense Debit		Payable Credit	of Bonds Payable
			(B - C)	(E + D)

c.   **GENERAL JOURNAL**

DATE (or entry no.)	ACCOUNT TITLES AND EXPLANATION	POST. REF.	DEBIT	CREDIT

a.   **STOVALL COMPANY**

b.   Premium Amortization Schedule

(A)	(B)	(C)	(D)	(E)
Interest	Bond Interest	Cash Credit	Premium on Bonds	Carrying Value
Payment Date	Expense Debit		Payable Debit	of Bonds Payable
			(B - C)	(E - D)

c.   **GENERAL JOURNAL**

DATE (or entry no.)	ACCOUNT TITLES AND EXPLANATION	POST. REF.	DEBIT	CREDIT

a.   **GOODHEW SOFTWARE SYSTEMS, INC.**

Discount Amortization Schedule

(A)	(B)	(C)	(D)	(E)
Interest	Bond Interest	Cash Credit	Discount on Bonds	Carrying Value
Payment Date	Expense Debit		Payable Credit	of Bonds Payable
			(B - C)	(E + D)

GOODHEW SOFTWARE SYSTEMS, INC.
b.   **GENERAL JOURNAL**

DATE (or entry no.)	ACCOUNT TITLES AND EXPLANATION	POST. REF.	DEBIT	CREDIT

a.   **KELLY FURNITURE COMPANY**

Premium Amortization Schedule

(A)	(B)	(C)	(D)	(E)
Interest	Bond Interest	Cash Credit	Premium on Bonds	Carrying Value
Payment Date	Expense Debit		Payable Debit	of Bonds Payable
			(B - C)	(E - D)

KELLY FURNITURE COMPANY
GENERAL JOURNAL

b.

DATE (or entry no.)	ACCOUNT TITLES AND EXPLANATION	POST. REF.	DEBIT	CREDIT

Problem 15-6 or 15-6A

a.

Name_____

_____

GENERAL JOURNAL

DATE (or entry no.)		ACCOUNT TITLES AND EXPLANATION	POST. REF.	DEBIT	CREDIT

b. _____ **COMPANY** _____

Partial Balance Sheet

September 30, 200__

Current liabilities:		

Long-term liabilities:		

Business Decision Case 15-1   Name _____

	Alternative (1)	Alternative (2)

Business Decision Case 15-2

a.
_____
_____
_____
_____

b.
_____
_____
_____
_____

c.
_____
_____
_____
_____
_____

Name_____

_____

a.

_____
_____
_____
_____
_____
_____
_____
_____
_____
_____

b.

_____
_____
_____
_____
_____
_____
_____
_____
_____
_____
_____

c.

_____
_____
_____
_____
_____
_____
_____
_____
_____
_____
_____
_____
_____

Annual Report Analysis 15-4

Company	Income before Interest and Taxes (Operating Income)	Interest Expense	Times Interest Earned Ratio

Annual Report Analysis 15-5

Name _____

a. _____

_____

_____

_____

b. _____

_____

_____

_____

_____

Ethics–Writing Experience 15-6

a. _____

b. _____

c. _____

_____

_____

_____

_____

_____

_____

d. _____

_____

_____

_____

_____

_____

_____

e. _____

_____

_____

_____

_____

_____

_____

_____

Exercise 16-1

_____
_____
_____
_____
_____
_____
_____
_____

Exercise 16-2

	Accrual Basis	Add	Deduct	Cash Basis

Exercise 16-3

	Add	Deduct

Exercise 16-4

Exercise 16-5

Exercise 16-6

Exercise 16-7

Exercise 16-8

QUALITY MERCHANDISE, INC.
Statement of Cash Flows
For the Year Ended December 31, 2000

Cash flows from operating activities:

Cash flows from investing activities:

Cash flows from financing activities:

Increase in cash

Supplemental cash flow information:

Exercise 16-9

Working Paper to Convert Income Statement From Accrual Basis to Cash Basis

For the Year Ended December 31, 1999

Accrual Basis	Add	Deduct	Cash Basis

b.

Partial Statement of Cash Flows
For the Year Ended December 31, 1999

c.

Partial Statement of Cash Flows
For the Year Ended December 31, 1999

Statement of Cash Flows
For the Year Ended December 31, 2000

Cash flows from operating activities:

Cash flows from investing activities:

Cash flows from financing activities:

Problem 16-4 or 16-4A   Name _____

a. _____

b. _____

c. _____

d. _____

e. _____

Problem 16-5 or 16-5A

a.

Name_____

_____

_____, INC.

Working Paper for Statement of Cash Flows

For the Year Ended June 30, 2000

	Account Balance 6/30/99	Analysis of Transactions for the Year Ended 6/30/00		Account Balance 6/30/00
		Debit	Credit	
Debits				
Credits				

	Account Balance 6/30/99	Analysis of Transactions for the Year Ended 6/30/00		Account Balance 6/30/00
		Debit	Credit	
Cash Flows from Operating Activities:				
Cash Flows from Investing Activities:				
Cash Flows from Financing Activities:				
Noncash Financing and Investing Activities:				

Problem 16-5 or 16-5A (concluded)
b.

Name _____

_____

Statement of Cash Flows
For the Year Ended June 30, _____

Cash flows from operating activities:

Cash flows from investing activities:

Cash flows from financing activities:

Schedule of noncash investing and financing activities:

Supplemental cash flow information:

NATIONAL SPORTS, INC.

Statement of Cash Flows

For the Year Ended December 31, 2000

Cash flows from operating activities:

Cash flows from investing activities:

Cash flows from financing activities:

Schedule of noncash investing and financing activities:

Supplemental cash flow information:

HARDIPLANK SIDING, INC.
Schedule of Cash Flows from Operating Activities
For the Year Ended December 31, 2000

a.

b.

c.

d.

e.

f.

g.

h.

i.

Annual Report Analysis 16-5   Name _____

_____

a.

Company	Net Cash Provided by Operating Activities	Average Number of Shares of Common Stock Outstanding	Cash-Flow per Share

b.

Company	Net Cash Provided by Operating Activities	Net Sales	Cash-Flow Margin

c.

Company	Cash, Marketable Securities, & Net Cash Provided by Operating Activities	Current Liabilities	Cash-Flow Liquidity Ratio

BOSTON COMPANY

Comparative Income Statements

For the Years Ended December 31, 2000 and 1999

	Year Ended December 31,		Increase or (Decrease) 2000 over 1999		Percentage of Net Sales December 31	
	(1) 2000	(2) 1999	(3) Dollars	(4) Percent	(5) 2000	(6) 1999

Exercise 17-2

Exercise 17-3

a.

b.

Exercise 17-4

Exercise 17-5

Exercise 17-6

Name _____

Exercise 17-7

_____
_____
_____
_____
_____
_____
_____

Exercise 17-8

_____
_____
_____
_____
_____
_____
_____
_____

Exercise 17-9

_____
_____
_____
_____
_____
_____
_____

Exercise 17-10

_____
_____
_____
_____
_____
_____
_____
_____
_____

Exercise 17-11

_____
_____
_____
_____
_____
_____
_____

Exercise 17-12

a._____

_____
_____
_____

b._____

_____
_____
_____

Exercise 17-13

_____
_____
_____
_____
_____
_____
_____
_____
_____
_____

Consolidated Statement of Earnings

For the Years Ended December 31, 1995 and 1994

(in thousands, except per data share)

	December 31		Horizontal Analysis Increase or (Decrease) 1995 over 1994		Vertical Analysis Percent of Net Sales December 31	
	(1) 1995	(2) 1994	(3) Dollars	(4) Percent	(5) 1995	(6) 1994

Consolidated Balance Sheets

For the Years Ended December 31, 1995 and 1994

(dollars in thousands)

	December 31		Horizontal Analysis Increase or (Decrease) 1995 over 1994		Vertical Analysis Percent of Total Assets December 31	
	(1) 1995	(2) 1994	(3) Dollars	(4) Percent	(5) 1995	(6) 1994

Consolidated Balance Sheets

For the Years Ended December 31, 1995 and 1994

(dollars in thousands)

	December 31		Horizontal Analysis Increase or (Decrease) 1995 over 1994		Vertical Analysis Percent of Total Assets December 31	
	(1) 1995	(2) 1994	(3) Dollars	(4) Percent	(5) 1995	(6) 1994

a.

FORD MOTOR COMPANY
Trend Analysis

	1993	1994	1995

b.

Problem 17-2A

a.

DEERE & COMPANY

Trend Analysis

	1992	1993	1994	1995

b.

Name_____

_____ **COMPANY**

	December 31	
	2000	1999
a.		
b.		
c.		
d.		
e.		

Calculations:

	Increase	Decrease	Unaffected
a. **Effect on amount of working capital**			
(1)			
(2)			
(3)			
(4)			
(5)			
(6)			
(7)			
(8)			
(9)			
(10)			
(11)			
(12)			
(13)			
(14)			
(15)			
b. **Effect on current ratio**			
(1)			
(2)			
(3)			
(4)			
(5)			
(6)			
(7)			
(8)			
(9)			
(10)			
(11)			
(12)			
(13)			
(14)			
(15)			

Problem 17-5

a.

	Company 1	Company 2	Company 3

b.

	Company 1	Company 2	Company 3

Name_____

_____

DIGITAL COMPANY

b.

	Effect on		
	Operating Margin	*Turnover of Operating Assets*	*Rate of Return on Operating Assets*

	1995	1994
a.		
b.		
c.		
d.		

a.

b.

c.

d.

e.

f.

g.

h.

i.

j.

_____**COMPANY**

a.

b.

_____

DARLING CORPORATION

a.

b.

c.

d.

MILLER MANUFACTURING COMPANY

a.

b.

ANALYSIS OF INVESTMENT ALTERNATIVES

	Apple, Inc.	Baker Co.	Cookie Corp.

b.

c.

Annual Report Analysis 17-4

a.

b.

c.

_____

_____

_____

_____

_____

_____

_____

_____

_____

_____

_____

_____

_____

_____

_____

_____

_____

_____

_____

_____

_____

_____

_____

_____

_____